Christmas in

Venezuela

By Christina Earley

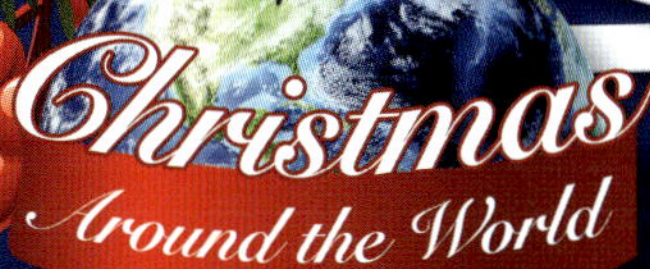

Table of Contents

A Starfish Book

Teaching Tips for Caregivers:

As a caregiver, you can help your child succeed in school by giving them a strong foundation in language and literacy skills and a desire to learn to read.

This book helps children grow by letting them practice reading skills.

Reading for pleasure and interest will help your child to develop reading skills and will give your child the opportunity to practice these skills in meaningful ways.

- Encourage your child to read on her own at home
- Encourage your child to practice reading aloud
- Encourage activities that require reading
- Establish a reading time
- Talk with your child
- Give your child writing materials

Teaching Tips for Teachers:

Research shows that one of the best ways for students to learn a new topic is to read about it.

Before Reading

- Read the "Words to Know" and discuss the meaning of each word.
- Read the back cover to see what the book is about.

During Reading

- When a student gets to a word that is unknown, ask them to look at the rest of the sentence to find clues to help with the meaning of the unknown word.
- Ask the student to write down any pages of the book that were confusing to them.

After Reading

- Discuss the main idea of the book.
- Ask students to give one detail that they learned in the book by showing a text dependent answer from the book.

Christmas in Venezuela

FELIZ NAVIDAD

Christmas is a special time in Venezuela.

The season is celebrated from December through February.

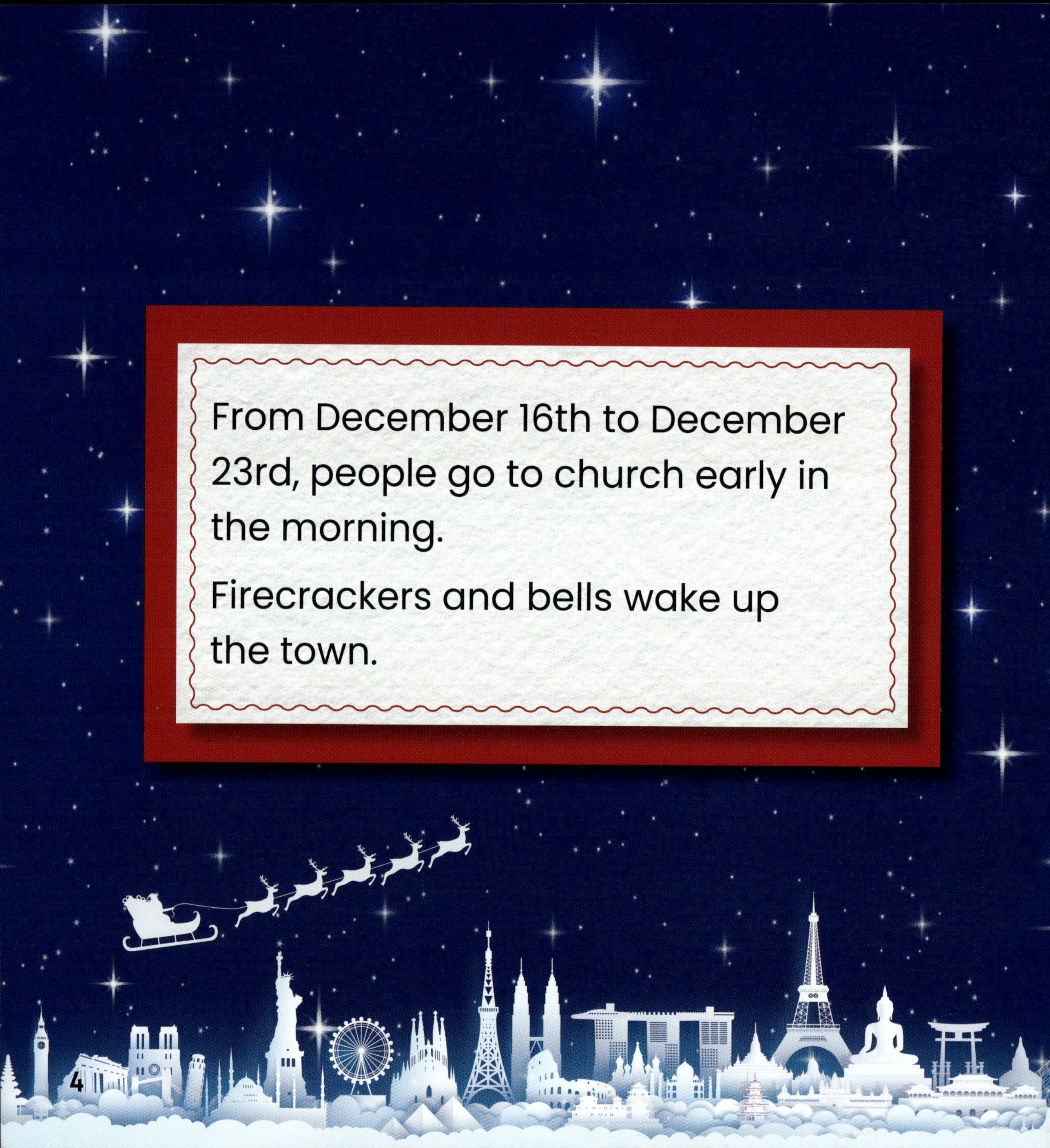

From December 16th to December 23rd, people go to church early in the morning.

Firecrackers and bells wake up the town.

Fun Fact:
Many people roller skate or ride bikes to attend these services.

Nativity scenes tell the story of Christmas.

These are called *nacimientos.*

Gaitas are Christmas songs with a fun beat.

Special guitars, drums, and **maracas** are played.

They make a joyful sound.

Fun Fact:
Gaita music combines Latin and African cultures.

Niño Jesús, or Baby Jesus, brings presents on Christmas Eve.

They are put by the nativity.

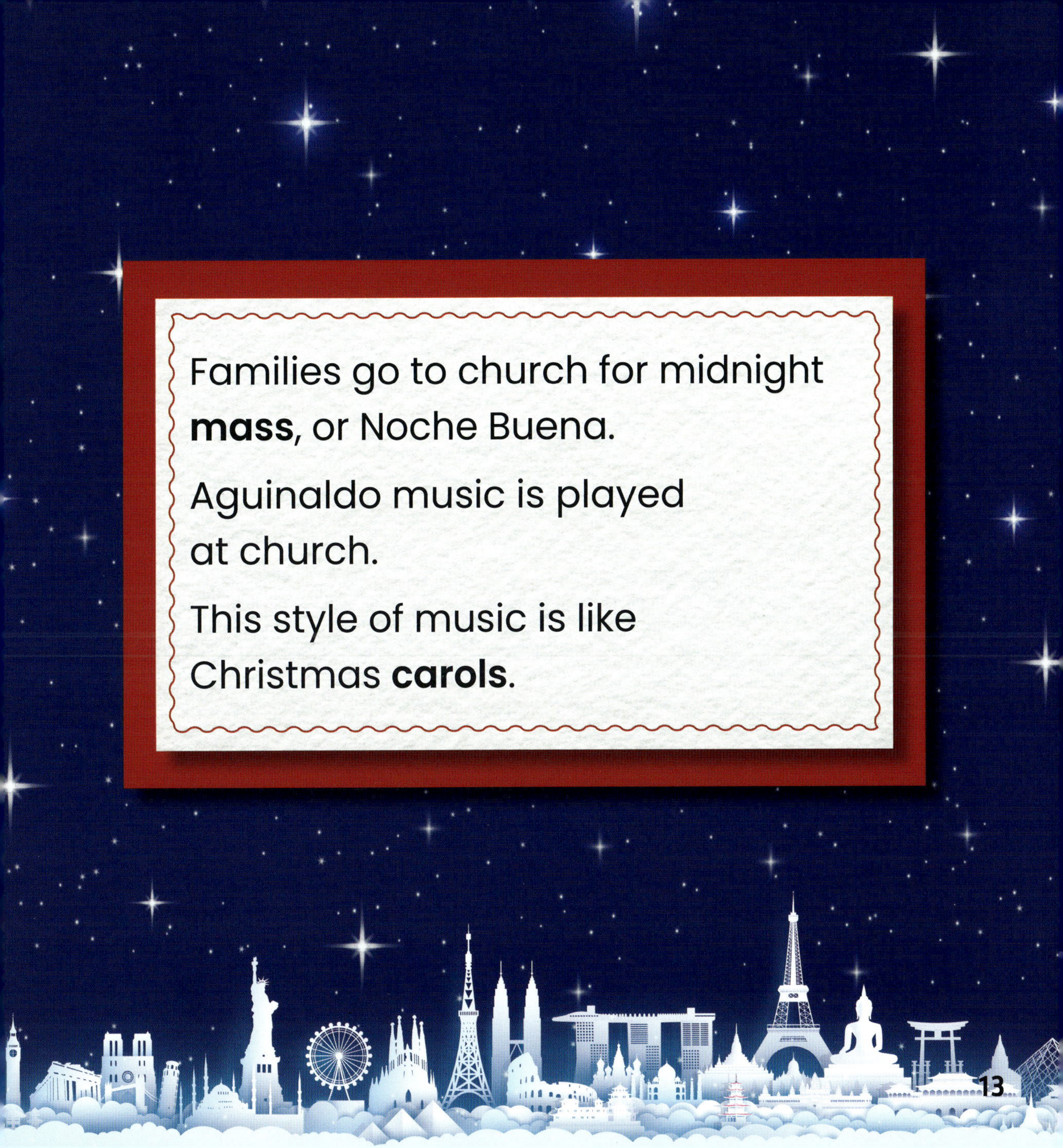

Families go to church for midnight **mass**, or Noche Buena.

Aguinaldo music is played at church.

This style of music is like Christmas **carols**.

After church, there is a party.

People dance and eat.

Hallacas are filled with meat and raisins.

They look like presents.

Fun Fact:
Hallacas are only eaten at Christmas because they take a long time to make.

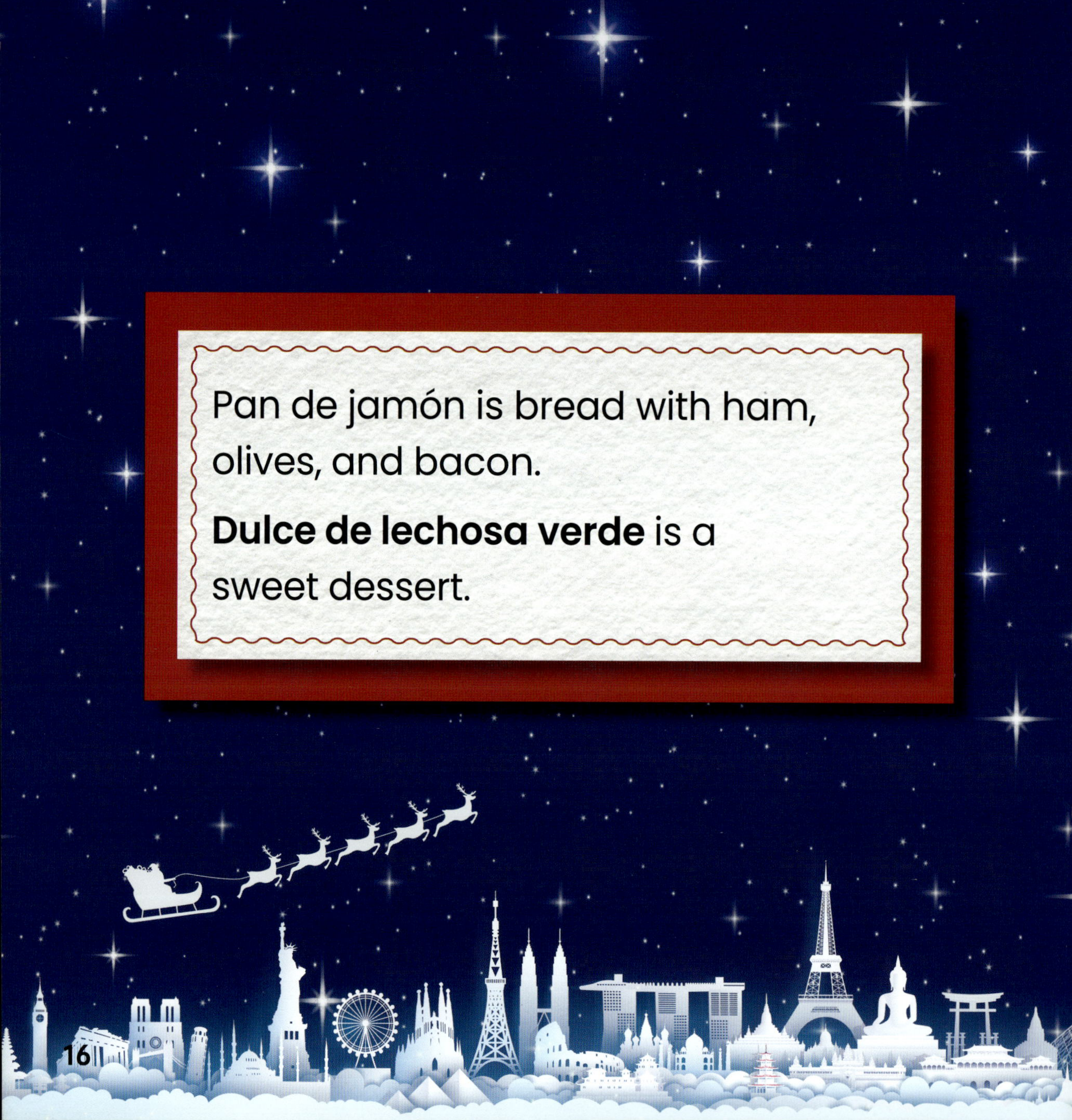

Pan de jamón is bread with ham, olives, and bacon.

Dulce de lechosa verde is a sweet dessert.

Pan de jamón

Many people decorate with lights.

Some have fake Christmas trees.

Craft: Maracas

Materials

- plastic Easter eggs (standard size)
- uncooked rice, dry beans, dry lentils, etc.
- plastic spoons
- patterned tape (washi tape)

Steps

1. Fill the eggs with dry ingredients.
2. Place the heads of two spoons facing each other. Use tape on the handles to secure together.
3. Slightly open the heads of the spoons. Put one egg inside with the wider part of the egg facing down toward the handles.
4. Wrap tape around the spoons at the seam of the egg to secure.
5. Continue to wrap tape around the head.

Recipe: Ensalada de Gallina (Chicken Salad)

Ingredients

- 2 uncooked chicken breasts (or precooked rotisserie chicken)
- 3 large potatoes, peeled and cubed
- 1 cup frozen peas and carrots
- 1 green apple, peeled and cubed
- 5 tablespoons mayonnaise
- 1 tablespoon vinegar
- salt to taste

Steps

1. Fill a large pot with water and heat to boiling. Add uncooked chicken breasts. Cook for about 20 minutes. Remove from water and shred into a small bowl. (If using precooked rotisserie chicken, skip the boiling and just shred.)
2. Fill a second large pot with water and heat to boiling. Add the cubed potatoes. After 10 minutes, add the frozen peas and carrots. Cook until fork-tender (about 5 additional minutes).
3. Drain the cooked mixed vegetables and put in a large bowl. Add the chicken. Cover and put in refrigerator to cool for an hour.
4. Add the apple, mayonnaise, and vinegar. Mix to coat. Add salt, if needed. Cover and refrigerate.

Words to Know

carols (KAR-uhlz): traditional, joyful songs, especially those sung at Christmas

dulce de lechosa verde (DUL-say day lech-OH-suh VAYR-day): a dessert made with green papaya, sugar, cloves, cinnamon, and pepper

hallacas (hal-LA-cas): thin layers of corn dough stuffed with meat, vegetables, and fruits, wrapped in plantain leaves, tied, and boiled

maracas (muh-RAH-kuz): musical instruments made from gourds filled with dried beans

mass (mas): a ritual of chants, prayers, readings, and songs in a church

nativity (nuh-TIV-i-tee): a stable scene that shows baby Jesus, Mary, Joseph, animals, shepherds, and angels

Index

Comprehension Questions

1. What are Christmas songs with a fun beat?
   a. nativities
   b. hallacas
   c. gaitas

2. Noche Buena is when families
   a. ride roller skates.
   b. go to church on Christmas Eve.
   c. put up the nativity.

3. Who gives presents to children?
   a. Baby Jesus
   b. Baby Jose
   c. Baby Julietta

4. True or false: Hallacas are only eaten at Christmas.

5. True or false: Presents are put outside the bedroom door.

Answers
1. c 2. b 3. a 4. True 5. False

About the Author

Christina Earley lives in South Florida with her with husband, son, and dog named Bailey. Her favorite holiday is Christmas because it is a magical time of year. She collects ornaments that remind her of special places and events. She and her family have lots of fun baking cookies and eating candy canes while looking at Christmas lights.

Written by: Christina Earley
Design by: Jen Bowers
Editor: Kim Thompson

Photographs: Cover ©2015 Paolo Costa/Shutterstock, pine ©Pasko Maksim/Shutterstock,world skyline©Painterstock/Shutterstock, background©ghenadie/Shutterstock, earth ©leonello/iStock; p.1 ©Mariana Mast/Shutterstock; p.3 ©2012 ESB Professional/ Shutterstock; p.5 ©2019 Moises Abraham/Shutterstock, ©2017 Michael C. Gray/Shutterstock, ornament©ekler/Shutterstock; p.7 ©2018 Rigucci/Shutterstock; p.9 ©2021 marinafrost/Shutterstock; p.11 ©2019 AnastasiaNi/Shutterstock, ©2014 glenda/Shutterstock; p.12 ©2017 Ian Dyball/Shutterstock; p.15 ©2020 SteAck/ Shutterstock; p.17 ©2016 acongar/Shutterstock, ©2019 CARLOS SANTOS RODAPEBR/Shutterstock; p.18 ©2014 Africa Team/ Shutterstock 2014 Africa Team/Shutterstock; p.20 ©2019 Olya Detry/Shutterstock; p.21 ©2019 FranciscoDania/Shutterstock

Library of Congress PCN Data
Christmas in Venezuela / Earley
Christmas Around the World
ISBN 978-1-63897-445-1 (hard cover)
ISBN 978-1-63897-560-1 (paperback)
ISBN 978-1-63897-675-2 (EPUB)
ISBN 978-1-63897-790-2 (eBook)
Library of Congress Control Number: 2022930314

Printed in the United States of America.

Seahorse Publishing Company
www.seahorsepub.com

Published in the United States
Seahorse Publishing
PO Box 771325
Coral Springs, FL 33077